T0171360

RADICAL LIVING AND GIVING

Saving, Spending, and Giving God's Way

SUELANGE MYERS

WESTBOW
PRESS
A DIVISION OF THOMAS NELSON

Scripture quotations are from the Holy Bible, New International Version®, NIV®. Copyright © 1973, 1978, 1984, 2011 by Biblica, Inc.™ Used by permission of Zondervan. All rights reserved worldwide. The "NIV" and "New International Version" are trademarks registered in the United States Patent and Trademark Office by Biblica, Inc.™

WestBow Press books may be ordered through booksellers or by contacting:

WestBow Press
A Division of Thomas Nelson
1663 Liberty Drive
Bloomington, IN 47403
www.westbowpress.com
1-(866) 928-1240

ISBN: 978-1-4497-9462-0 (sc)
ISBN: 978-1-4497-9461-3 (e)

Library of Congress Control Number: 2013908379

Printed in the United States of America.

WestBow Press rev. date: 05/20/2013

TABLE OF CONTENTS

"Command those who are rich in this present world not to be arrogant nor to put their hope in wealth, which is so uncertain, but to put their hope in God, who richly provides us with everything for our enjoyment. Command them to do good to be rich in good deeds, and to be generous and willing to share. In this way they will lay up a treasure for themselves as a firm foundation for the coming age, so that they may take hold of the life that is truly life."

—1 Timothy 6:17-19

INTRODUCTION

Money! We can't live with it and we can't live without it. We need it, we borrow it, we make it, and we steal it. It makes us, it breaks us, and it threatens to complicate us. We love it, we hate it, we give it, and we take it.

Money is a part of our lives and everything we do each day. The majority of our life is spent making and collecting money. The more we accumulate, the more we spend to fix and upgrade our accumulations. It is a never-ending cycle that is a part of us till the day we die. For some, life is only about money. For it is by material goods they measure their living. But as biblical Christians, how does God want us to handle the accumulation of money?

Is it wrong to accumulate money? The Bible teaches us to work hard and take care of our families. Can we help it that in the process of our hard work our success has brought us an accumulation of wealth? Once we accumulate wealth, is there a certain way the Lord would have us handle it? How much are we expected to give away?

You may be thinking something like this: "I have a heart to give, but I simply have nothing left to give after taking care of the needs of my family. God cannot expect me to give something that I do not have. Didn't He say He watched out for the sparrow? People are more important than birds, right? Should we have to be responsible for the needs of someone else? If we helped them, wouldn't that encourage them to become lazy? They should work for what they get just like I have."

Consider this, however: Is money consuming you and your time? Are you always worried about having enough? Do you have so much money that you spend all your time worrying about how to use it? It may be that you are stressed out in thinking about retirement accounts, college funds, and where to go on your next vacation. You may be obsessed with keeping up with your friends—wondering what car they just bought or who ate at the best restaurant in town. No matter what we do, money will always be a part of our lives.

We live in a world in which people either are inundated with money or are severely deficient when it comes to material gain. Both extremes reflect a dire need that can only be met in Christ. As believers we have already found the hope only Jesus can bring. Now it is time for us to lend a hand to others who are still looking for the hope.

It is not humanly possible to complete this enormous task if we are following the rest of the world, with our time and resources being constantly consumed by material gain. In order to help others, we must first get our own hearts and homes in order. We must be willing not just to know Jesus but also to live our lives with eternity in view by recognizing what our personal sacrifice might be in order to reach others for Him. "For where your treasure is, there your heart will be also" (Matt. 6:20).

In this book we will look at the issue of money in a whole new light. The Bible has things to say about saving, spending, and giving, whether you are living in plenty or in want. No matter what your financial situation may be, in this book you will learn how to live—so you can give again and again.

"No one can serve two masters. Either you will hate the one and love the other, or you will be devoted to the one and despise the other. You cannot serve both God and money."

—Matthew 6:24

CHAPTER 1

MONEY—ALWAYS AN ISSUE

From our earliest years we learn what we believe to be the purpose of money in our society. We watch our parents buy and sell things. We are given money ourselves as a reward, a gift, or perhaps as compensation for a job we performed. We see advertisements of what can be purchased if we simply have enough money. We begin to brag about our possessions and what we hope to possess in the future. As young children, we quickly learn to notice the biggest house in the neighborhood, the best toys, and the people we know who seem to get whatever their heart desires. Then we dream about all the things we plan to obtain when we grow up. Desires start to mount. We may want something so badly that we fall into coveting what the next person has—or even stealing it. We simply remain unsatisfied until we obtain what we want. It doesn't take long until we have become another American caught up in the never-ending cycle of materialism. Materialism, we ask? Yes, materialism is taking over in America.

So what is exactly is materialism? Can materialism be measured? Webster's dictionary tells us that materialism is "a preoccupation with or stress upon the material rather than intellectual or spiritual things." According to one common thesaurus, materialism is synonymous with greed and covetousness. It can also be considered an obsession toward material gain.

Maybe you're a little like me and think, "I am not greedy, and I don't covet what my neighbor has." Alright, think again. Consider whether you are being honest with yourself. Why do you have the things you have? Why do you do all the things you do? Is it because you need everything you have? It might not be absolutely essential that you go on that vacation. You might not "have to have" those special shoes, that additional purse, or the newest sports equipment. Do you really need a new computer every year? Obviously the list could go on and on. We should evaluate ourselves. Both our checkbook and our calendar are great indicators of how much we are consumed by accumulating material things.

Materialism has become a war that we are battling among and within ourselves. Which side are we on in this war? Can we ever win, or should we just back out? How can we escape once we are consumed by it all?

Most of us can recall stories we have been told by our parents and grandparents about the "good old days." Those were the days when living was simple and everyone was thankful for one another. Family, friends, and neighbors shared with one another and were a part of each other's lives. It did not matter what one's status may have been or what someone had. This interest was genuine: a true act of caring.

Sometime between then and now our culture has changed. Our freedom to flourish—monetarily and materially—has brought with it a great burden that most of us do not handle well. With a few exceptions, most of us have not only been affected by but also are a product of this shift toward materialism that has become all inclusive and all about "me." Everything we do is for gain, even what we used to do as simple acts of kindness. Now what has become foremost in our mind is "what will I get out of what I am about to do?" If I won't benefit from it, I probably won't participate in that event or complete that act. This affects who we associate with, the activities we involve ourselves in, and every other part of our lives.

Are we as Christians any different from the world? We need to each ask ourselves that question. Maybe we should take some time to look back on our own histories to see how materialism has insinuated its ugly head into our lives. On the other hand, maybe we can't tell when it started. Perhaps it was always there.

At this point, some may say this talk is all a bit extreme. Materialism likened to a battle or war? There must be more important issues with which to consume our time, right? Stop and think for just a moment on how money has affected you and your family. What about those around you? The reality is quite simple: "For the love of money is a root of all kinds of evil. Some people, eager for money, have wandered from the faith and pierced themselves with many griefs" (1 Tim. 6:10).

Let's consider the question, "Whose side am I on when it comes to the battle of materialism?" This all depends on whether you control the money or the money controls you. Are you so driven to obtain material goods that even the simplest of decisions is clouded by materialism's control over you? Or consider all the time you spend keeping up with your accumulations. What about building bigger barns just to store all your "stuff" as well as installing a security system to protect it? Not to mention all the time we spend shopping for our hobbies. If we evaluated where our priorities lie, what would the result be? Isn't it time to tip the balance in the opposite direction? We need to take the focus off of ourselves and put it on God by serving others.

Most of us have heard time and time again that money is the number one cause of divorce and family conflict. You do not have to look very far to find many people you know who have been affected by this very thing. Even the most well-meaning families have been torn with the issue of money. There is the time spent away from family to "provide for one's family." There is the issue of keeping up with the rest of the people you like to be with. And what about the phrase, "I deserve my fair share?"

At the end of the day, there is no measuring stick for materialism. However, the Bible is very clear: "To whom much is given, much will be required" (Luke 12:48).

In the story of the rich man and Lazarus, the rich man had accumulated great material wealth. Much was required of him to give to those around him in need (whether spiritual or material), like the poor beggar Lazarus. The rich man failed to do what was required of him and paid a dear price (Luke 16:19-31).

Aren't we like the rich man? We may not have the riches that he had acquired. But have we taken the time to evaluate our own lives to see if we are aware of those who are around us? Are we doing everything we can to be the stewards that God wants us to be?

Maybe it is time for us to get back to the "good old days." It may require immense changes in areas in which it is difficult to let go. But I for one am not ready to pay a dear price for ignoring what God has called me to do. I am ready to be relieved of the things that might cause me to wander away from my faith. Just maybe, others around me may follow my example, or the ultimate example, Jesus.

STUDY QUESTIONS ▉▉▉▉▉▉▉▉▉▉▉▉▉▉▉▉▉

1. What is the purpose of money?

2. What is materialism? How does it personally affect you and your family?

3. What does the Bible teach us about money in Matthew 6:24?

4. Can you think of a situation—perhaps involving someone you know—in which the love of money has caused disaster or ruin? (Refer to 1 Tim. 6:10.)

5. What lessons can be learned concerning the rich man and Lazarus? (See Luke 16:19-31.)

"Fill the earth and subdue it."

—Genesis 1:28

CHAPTER 2

STEWARDSHIP—
WHAT GOD HAS IN MIND!

In order to comprehend the topics of money and giving, we need to understand the biblically based concept of *stewardship*. Webster defines a steward in the secular sense as "a person morally responsible for the careful use of money, time, talents, and other resources." According to *Holman Bible Dictionary*, New Testament stewardship suggests that time, talents, and material possessions, or wealth are used for the service of God.[1] That dictionary also states that a biblical worldview of stewardship includes "utilizing and managing all resources God provides for the glory of God and the betterment of His creation." Another source states that stewards should be considered to "act as managers who have the authority to run everything as God planned."[2]

---

[1] *Holman Bible Dictionary,* ed. Butler C. Trent (Broadman & Holman, 1991), s.v. "stewardship." http://www.studylight.org/dic/hbd/view.cgi?w=stewardship.

[2] Earl Radmacher, Ron Allen, and H. Wayne House, *Nelson's Compact Bible Commentary* (Nashville, TN: Nelson Reference & Electronic, 2004), 2.

Does the Bible actually teach this lifestyle as something we should embrace in the twenty first century?

While there are many references to support this claim, there is one that sums it up clearly: "The earth is the Lord's and everything in it, the world, and all who live in it" (Ps. 24:1). In the beginning God gave Adam and Eve the responsibility to subdue the earth (see Gen. 1). This responsibility has been passed on to each and every one of us across the generations of time. God made the world; He put us in dominion over it; and we are to take care of every single person and thing.

Stop and ponder that a moment. So the earth is the Lord's, and everything in it belongs to Him. Obviously that includes me, my next door neighbor, and even that guy over there in Africa. Having dominion over the world means I should be concerned about more than saving the whales and not polluting the ozone layer. I need to be focused on people—real people with real needs. If I want to do things God's way, I cannot limit my concerns to my own isolated community. I am responsible for so much more.

Whether we think of it or not, we are responsible for how we do things. What if we do not choose to use every talent God has given us or think about each purchase we make? It is not about "me." It is about Him (Jesus). It is about other people that need both physical and spiritual healing.

Many of us are in denial that we live in one the greatest countries of plenty. Even those on the poorest end of the spectrum in the Western world are wealthier than most people in the rest of the world. Most of the people in Third World nations could live on what we in the Western world throw away each day.

So why are we throwing so much away? For some of us, it is because we lack the space in our walk-in closet or our three-car garage. Maybe it is because we don't like something as we originally thought we might; now it is seen as a piece of "junk." Sometimes the complaint is that it isn't as easy to use as described in the advertisement. Regardless of the reason, this is becoming a considerable problem in America. This is one crisis that can be solved by simply being careful making purchasing choices, and more importantly, finding alternatives to throwing things away. We need to consider that oftentimes God provides for people by means of other people.

Spending some time in a Third World country can be helpful for observing the actual needs of very poor people. My first real exposure to extreme poverty was on a trip to Cambodia, which at the time was the poorest country in Asia. Right from my landing in this nation, I knew I was going to be in shock. I could see very few lights at night. Yet I was landing in the capital city of Phnom Penh, which had well over one million people.

Since we were part of a mission trip, we stayed on a compound where church services and children's ministries were held (which was a better accommodation than most). We were given three one-liter bottles of water a day to use to clean ourselves. The local water from the tap was so contaminated that those of us not immune to its germs could get sick from exposing it to our skin. There were no screens on the windows, which meant that geckos were everywhere. Have you ever tried to go to sleep at night with lizards on the ceiling above your bed? I spent several nights wondering if they would suddenly loosen themselves and plunge, landing on my body. Amazingly, though, they didn't fall too often. The temperature there is between 80 and 100 degrees year round. Dirt was everywhere, so I never felt really clean (so much for those three bottles of water).

There was no air conditioning in the excruciating heat. The marketplace flies were all over the meat! Seeing enough of this made me want to be a vegetarian.

God had sent me to this country to minister to the people. I had thought that meant bringing them to a saving knowledge of Him. But how could I do that when all around me was such poverty? Small clapboard huts were everywhere in the city, made out of whatever materials could be rummaged. Outside of them stood little children, some poorly clad and others with no clothing at all. Of course many of them were dirty, having little running water, and dirty water at that. They were mostly hungry and would beg whenever I (a foreigner) would walk by. In fact I have been to many countries before and since, and I have yet to see so many "truly needy beggars" in one place. We also had the opportunity to spend some time in remote areas.

The poverty persisted everywhere we went. We often handed out items: used clothing, toothbrushes, and snacks. The people took anything that was given. You knew it was going to be used for some good purpose. We (I and the team I was with) made a small difference in each place on the days we were there. But the experience made a large difference in my life and still affects me more than a decade later.

Fast forward a few years to when my husband and I had an opportunity to spend a year teaching English in Mongolia. This was the third poorest country in Asia. Yet this became our home for many months.

We spent a year in what I would call primitive camping conditions. To the Mongolians, however, we were wealthy. We lived in a two-bedroom home. This home had no kitchen sink; water had to be hauled and boiled for all kitchen and cooking tasks. The floors were wooden and had large gaps covered by cardboard with a piece of carpet thrown on top.

Because of this we had many mice all the time. I am not sure which is better, the fear of geckos crawling on you in your bed or mice? The floor was also cold most of the time, since Mongolia's winters are extreme, reaching 50-60 degrees below zero. The heating and electric utilities provided service inconsistently throughout our town. There were electricity blackouts, often at the most random of times. Heating was available only from September 15 to May 15. Never mind that we had blizzards before and after those dates and still had no heat or electricity at times.

There were other challenges of everyday living also. Mongolia is known for its dust storms, especially in the Gobi Desert region. I had never seen anything like them in my life. You can imagine what they do to clothing. I would use a very small wringer washer and wash one pair of my husband's jeans three times before the dirt would be out of them.

All of our shopping required long walks or trips to town and hauling whatever we needed, if we could find it. We were limited to about five types of veggies and one type of fruit in our town. During that year, Asia was dealing with the bird flu, so very few eggs could be found. We did purchase a few foreign food products at astronomical prices, but in general, our diet was quite limited. We lost a great deal of weight. It was easy for each of us to fit inside the extra layers of clothing that we packed on and even wore indoors during the winter months.

There is so much more that could be said about residing in this nation of Mongolia and how it changed our thoughts about life and living. But there is something greater that I learned from these people as well. On a few occasions we had an opportunity to visit other Mongolian homes, namely gers (felt-covered tent homes). These homes were very simply furnished: a couple beds (which also served for sitting), a stove for heating and cooking, and perhaps a chest or two for storing things. Whenever we went into these homes, even as complete strangers, we were welcomed. We were given a seat and something to eat or drink, even if it meant that they would go without food to serve their guest. This was part of the culture, even among the poorest of the poor. They treated everyone as part of their family, considering it their responsibility to share with others in any way they could. They would pool together family resources to send someone to school or to get a family member a car. Yet these people were not believers or followers of Christ. Most of them did not have a Bible and did not know what it said about helping others.

God has placed in each of our hearts this same desire to help others. We (ourselves and our culture) have suppressed that desire and have changed it to seeking to meet our own needs and wants. We have forgotten about our God-given responsibility to subdue the earth and to use our time, talents, material possessions, and wealth in furthering His kingdom. We have become like the rich young man who was unwilling to sell all he had to give money to the poor and follow Jesus (Matt. 19:16-23).

I challenge you today to get out of your "me zone" and head to a Third World nation. Your eyes will forever be opened to others the way God intended them to be in the first place. Let Him work on your heart to envision the needs of others and to see that our job is more than just saving the whales and keeping the ozone layer pure. There are real people out there with real needs, and yet they seem to understand stewardship better than you and I do. When all this stuff you currently possess gets stripped away, you too will be able to see more clearly. Take off your rose-colored glasses and get yourself a new prescription from God Himself.

STUDY QUESTIONS

1. Define stewardship.

2. How does Genesis 1:28 relate to stewardship?

3. What does Psalm 24:1 teach about stewardship?

4. What is our personal responsibility when it comes to stewardship?

5. What can you do to become more aware of the needs of others?

6. Have you ever considered doing something radical for Jesus? Consider Matthew 19:16-23.

7. Are you still living in your "me zone" and wearing those rose-colored glasses?

"For whoever has will be given more and they will
have an abundance. Whoever does not have, even
what they have will be taken away from them."
—Matthew 25:29

CHAPTER 3

WHY SHOULD I GIVE THE MOST I CAN?

By now we could probably agree that money itself is not the problem in our society. It is us: the spenders of the money. The crisis is related to our misconception of the purpose of money. This takes us to the human nature issue. When God is not the authority in our lives, everything is about "me." I need to please myself. I want to be comfortable. I deserve the best. I worked for it—therefore it is mine. I can't trust anyone else with my stuff. My success is measured by what I possess.

If we honestly evaluated ourselves, most of these thoughts have at least crossed our mind, if not dictated the way we live. And why not? This is what society teaches us through every avenue in the media and especially among those we rub shoulders with each day. Why is it that we who live in America (or Canada and Europe), possessing most of the world's wealth, do so little to help those who do not get a chance to become self-sufficient?

You may wonder, "What can I do about it? Even if I change myself and how I live, what difference would that really make?" In all likelihood, you already do some things for others sometimes. You give when non-profit agencies call your home for donations. You give food to your local food pantry. You even tithe to your local church (which is already better than most churchgoers). But the question you should ask yourself is how much money is left after doing all these things? How much does God expect us to give?

Do you really want to know the answer to this question? Are you ready to take the plunge, or would it be better to ease into it? In my experience, most people work better in a progression mode. Let's start small. What is the minimum that God requires of me? No, that doesn't seem to sound right. Am I really going to tell God that I am only going to do the minimum of what He requires of me? In most areas of our lives we will find little success with that motto. Yet that is what most of us are doing and how we think when it comes to the area of money and giving. It is time to get more serious. So, what does God want me to do with my money?

First of all, we must get rid of the phrase "my money." Everything we are and have belongs to God (see Ps. 24:1). We were only given money to see how we would utilize it, just as in the parable of the ten talents (see Matt. 25:14-30). The more you have, the more you are accountable for. Each of us was given a great responsibility from the first man, Adam. "Be fruitful and increase in number; fill the earth and subdue it" (Gen. 1:28a). This meant that God chose man to oversee the planet and all that is in it (aren't we all glad for the increase of population to take on that great task!). We are to act as managers who have the authority to run everything as God planned.[3] Each and every day we are

_____

[3] Radmacher, Allen, and House, *Nelson's Compact Bible Commentary*, 2.

held accountable as stewards of this earth. We will be judged on how we subdue it.

Since the earth is the Lord's and everything in it, we must reprioritize our selfish way of thinking. God holds "me" responsible to take care of the earth and the people around me, as much as I am able. This is something that God has asked me to do as a believer until the day He calls me home. It will not look the same for everyone. Again, "To whom much is given, much will be required" (Luke 12:48). As already mentioned, the example of the rich man and Lazarus (Luke 16:19-31) shows what God expects of us. This may seem dramatic, since many do not fall into the same category of living as the rich man.

What about James 1:27? It says, "Religion that God our Father accepts as pure and faultless is this: to look after orphans and widows in their distress [take care of their physical needs] and to keep oneself from being polluted by the world [being overtaken by materialism]." Ouch! This verse speaks to all of us, no matter what our monetary status is currently or will be in the future. To varying degrees, most of us fall into one or both of the categories mentioned here in James. As you go through your day, take a moment to pause for a time of prayer and contemplation. We need to earnestly seek Him and ask Him to show us what we should be doing to put James 1:27 into practice every day.

If we let the words of James 1:27 and their implication really sink in, it can be overwhelming. How can I be responsible for widows and orphans? And that is just a starting point. That still leaves the needs of the rest of the world. First, it will take a true purging—to become unpolluted by the world—to even recognize that others have needs. Until then, we may be too caught up with "me."

As we study the Bible in the area of giving, we can see the importance God placed on both giving and sharing. God's Word is very blunt on this issue. He expects us to give. In the book of Malachi, God is speaking to His people about this: "Will a man rob God? Yet you rob Me. "But you ask, 'How do we rob you?' "In tithes and offerings. You are under a curse—the whole nation of you because you are robbing Me" (Mal. 3:8-9). Tithe may be a familiar term to most of us. It was accepted in the Old Testament as 10 percent of whatever one had to give (see Lev. 27). Although it still might be a stretch for most believers, God's expectations did not end with 10 percent as those Old Testament believers had been taught. He was preparing them to increase their measure of giving the more He revealed to them.

In the New Testament, we see Jesus teaching His followers to step it up a notch. He shares the story about the widow's offering. She gave all that she had (see Luke 21:1-4). Later, in the Acts of the Apostles, we see the early church believers sharing all their possessions and being recognized for doing so. "All the people were one in heart and mind. No one claimed that any of his possessions was his own, but they shared everything they had . . . There were no needy persons from among them. From time to time those who owned lands or houses sold them, brought the money from the sales and put it at the apostle's feet, and it was distributed to anyone as he had need" (Acts 4:32-37). As a result of this, "The Lord added to their number daily those who were being saved" (Acts 2:47b).

Wow! Giving away everything and sharing everything we have is a concept we cannot wrap our minds around. We may still be stuck on that 10 percent dilemma. We try to fight, scream, cry, and argue our way out of that 10 percent that we deem is ours. Yes, ours! We are such selfish creatures. Most of us are light years away from sharing all we have, if indeed that is what we are supposed to do. Unfortunately, many of us have become a product of our society. We have been taught that everything we make or collect is our very own.

So the question is, "Why should I give the most I can?" In order to answer this, we will have to return to the term stewardship and its meaning, especially in regard to wealth and possessions.

If God has placed you in a developed country, He has allowed your needs to be met above and beyond. You probably have sufficient education or training that was provided to you, and you most likely have a decent paying job. If so, always remember God has called you as a person to work to the best of your ability (see Col. 3:23). If you have a chance to work your way up the ladder in your job, by all means do so. We do not have to stay at minimum wage labor. We can barely help ourselves with that kind of pay, let alone begin thinking of aiding others. God has called us to achieve to our fullest potential using our time and talents. However, you have to keep your motives in check along the way. The higher up the ladder most people get, the further from God and others they seem to be. Thus we have the scenarios concerning the rich and their disconnection from God and others. If our focus remains on God, we are well on the way to becoming the stewards God wants us to be.

We will never understand on this side of eternity why God has allowed certain people to be born in rags and others in riches. However, God has never intended the riches of one man to be hoarded while others are suffering with no way out. By this I am referring to the people living in Third World countries who are daily conducting back-breaking labor and receiving only one or two dollars a day. These are the people who cannot afford the materials to build a church or purchase their own Bibles, let alone pay a pastor. They are barely surviving and cannot even afford their most basic needs and that of their families. In such places the expansion of the kingdom of God might come to a halt without our financial assistance. We should ask this: Am I doing anything to help with foreign missions? What am I doing to combat world hunger? Have I ever gone without anything in order for someone else to have something? For some of us, the answers to these questions would be no. No is not the answer God wants to hear from us.

God, in His divine mercy, has allowed many of us to be born and raised in prosperous nations, such as the United States and Canada. But the question, "Why has God placed us here?" is long overdue. Was it to have every comfort and luxury on a daily basis? Come on now, what does He want you to do with what He has given you? What does He want you to physically do to advance His kingdom? What does He expect you to do in relieving the needs of the helpless and homeless and the orphans and widows? What about the lost? There is no one set answer for everyone. God asks different things of different people. However, we are called upon to sacrifice.

At this point some of you may be thinking, "Whew! You are not talking to me. I am not really rich, and I am giving my 10 percent. Surely I am good to go." But have you considered your time and your resources? What are you doing when you are not on your day job? Could you use more of your free time furthering God's kingdom, rather than buffing and waxing your second or third car or seeing that new movie? For others who might be on a fixed income and live from paycheck to paycheck, it may be all you have monetarily. However, you can still answer the question,

"Am I doing the most I can?" God may be calling you to do something different than what you are currently doing.

I must admit, what I am about to say will be considered very radical even by most of my family, friends, and acquaintances. Let me suggest it is time for you to reevaluate your life. A place to start is by making a new budget for your family, one that is based on only your basic needs. First Timothy 6:8-9 teaches us: "If we have food and clothing we will be content with that. Those who want to get rich fall into temptation and a trap and into many foolish and harmful desires that plunge people into ruin and destruction. For the love of money is the root of all kinds of evil. Some people, eager for money, have wandered from the faith and pierced themselves with many griefs." Instead of raising your budget with your income as most people are in the habit of doing, only raise it to meet increases in the costs of your basic needs (i.e., rises in prices of gas, food, etc.). I am suggesting that through His Word, God indicates that He expects us to give the rest of it to Him to foster and further here on earth His kingdom, which lasts for eternity.

My husband and I believe this to be the biblical model of giving and have adopted it as our own. We have taken the challenge to give the most we can of our time, our talents, and of course our resources. I can honestly say that we are not yet where we would like to be. However, we are strongly headed in the right direction with this model of giving.

From my own experience, let me suggest we do not need nearly as much as we think we do. You can have the willpower to say no to that new article of clothing since you have more than enough in your closet (this is most of us). Ask yourself, do you really need another magazine subscription? What about specialty coffees? And do you really need steak and ribs twice a week? These are just the everyday miniscule issues. What about the more important things? How much money you should have in your retirement account? Which car you should drive? Where should you send your child to college?

This is a whole new way of thinking and acting for most of us. But it is one that is necessary if we intend to follow God's instructions for being the stewards He has called us to be. If we fail in our stewardship, who will be able to take care of the least of these? Jesus says, "Whatever you did for one of the least of these brothers of mine, you did it for me" (Matt. 24:40). Jesus clearly placed an importance on "the least of these." Those who are part of "the least of these" are real people. Though they are more commonly found in Third World nations, there are many of "the least of these" right where you and I live.

In the next chapter, I will share with you how we as a couple embarked on this new lifestyle, and I will give you many tips on how you can make the changes too.

STUDY QUESTIONS

1. How much does God expect us to give? (Refer to Matt. 25:29.)

2. Summarize Psalm 24:1 in your own words.

3. What is the relationship between stewardship and giving the most I can?

4. According to James 1:27, what is our responsibility?

5. According to the Old Testament, what was a tithe? (See Lev. 27.)

6. What does the New Testament teach about tithing and giving in general? (See Luke 21:1-4; Acts 4:32-37.)

7. What command does God give us in Colossians 3:23?

8. What am I doing with my money? What is God calling me to do with my money?

9. What does 1 Timothy 6:8-9 teach about contentment?

10. Who are "the least of these" around you? What are you doing for them?

"Give, and it will be given to you. A good measure, pressed
down, shaken together and running over, will be poured into your
lap. For with the measure you use, it will be measured to you."
—Luke 6:38

CHAPTER 4

❖

GIVE TILL IT HURTS—BIBLICAL SACRIFICIAL GIVING

One day driving home, I was listening to a Christian radio station. They were having their biannual pledge drive to fund their operational costs. During that time someone called in and shared that God was instructing them to give their whole bank account to the ministry of the station. That may have been five dollars or fifty thousand dollars. The amount the person had in his bank account did not really matter in this situation—it was the response that God was looking for. As I was listening to this, it was a time of reflection for me. I was good at giving, I thought, but maybe I still had a long way to go. Even though I did not know what was in that person's bank account, I did know what was in mine. After all I had learned about money and giving, was I still trying to cling to what was mine?

Most of us have heard various stories about the Great Depression and war times when there were food shortages, droughts, and other deprivations. People in those situations knew what it was like to go hungry or even go without basic needs such as shoes. God has blessed so many of us here in the Western world with the freedoms and opportunities to gain wealth. However, in the midst of all this gain, we forget we have the freedom to give. Stop telling yourself it is the responsibility of another. If God has blessed you by allowing you to be here at this time in history, and you have some material goods, you have a responsibility.

So how can we give sacrificially? We can follow Christ's example: "Foxes have holes, birds of the air have nests, but the Son of Man has no place to lay His head" (Matt. 7:20). Jesus first gave up heaven temporarily to come to earth for us. Can you imagine the contrast? He was willing to come to earth in a time of history when basic living was very difficult and civil unrest was commonplace. Additionally, He had to deal with being Jewish (the hated race). To top it all off, He left the security of His earthly home, where He likely had a stable income in a family-owned carpenter shop, to become an itinerant preacher. He had no home, and it seems he rarely knew where money and food might come from. It is probably not a stretch to guess that Jesus spent many nights with no roof over His head, hence the phrase, "nowhere to lay His head." Jesus did all this for us, in preparation for His death and resurrection. Can any of us deny that Jesus gave until it hurt?

What about the apostle Paul? He had been a well-known Pharisee who seemed quite successful in his own right. He probably came from a wealthy family, based on his references to his tutelage under Gamaliel, a leading teacher of the Jewish law. However, when Jesus called Paul, he willingly left his life of power, prestige, and comfort to teach the gospel message of Jesus. Paul also underwent some serious deprivation and persecution to remain a pillar of the early church that God wanted him to be (see 2 Cor. 11:23-29). Can we deny that the apostle Paul gave until it hurt?

Jesus and Paul were great role models of giving. They gave continuously, even when it hurt, sometimes for long periods of time. Where are we in this process? Maybe we have never even started. Perhaps we can begin learning about sacrificial giving by starting off small. What can we do without today? We can start by following the example of the young boy who willingly gave his small lunch to Jesus, just a little bit of fish and bread. In that time in history, it was possibly all he would get to eat for that day (see Matt. 14:13-21). However, he gave it up willingly to Jesus. How many of us would give up our lunch, grand or not? Such an act would be difficult for us, even though most of us will have the opportunity to eat later in the day. What about the coat on your back? What about the seat on the bus? Think of something we want here and now, and look around—you may see someone else who needs it more than you do.

I remember the time I was in Cambodia among the beggars. By America's standards, just about everyone could be considered a beggar. I remember having passed out all the gum, candy, and coins and smaller bills from my purse. There were just so many of these people asking for help. Some of them had more severe needs than others (hunger, lack of clothing, sickness). I was at the point that if I gave anything else it would hurt. Yet I was not quite willing to give all my lunch to Jesus. Little did I know that God would use this to teach me a lesson I am now sharing with you. Sometimes I wish I had the opportunity to return in this capacity to such a place. Looking back, what would have happened if I had given all my lunch to Jesus when I walked down those streets in Cambodia?

So far we have examined our role as stewards in regard to making and saving money. We know we are responsible to give as well. But most of us are still millions of miles away

27

from giving till it hurts. This is not about tithing, and it is not always about money. It is about our willingness to let go of what we think is ours and move from the place where everything is still about me. Am I willing to take something used in order for someone else to have something new? Am I willing to go without lunch so someone can have their only meal of the day? Am I willing to share Christ's love by giving unconditionally and sacrificially in any way He has called me to?

People everywhere are looking for hope, waiting for needs to be fulfilled. They just might be waiting for someone like you to be the hands and feet of Jesus. God blessed the little boy's lunch in such a radical, miraculous way. I wonder what He is going to do through your sacrifice as well as mine. What are you waiting for?

STUDY QUESTIONS

1. Is it necessary to give until it hurts? (See Matt. 7:20; 2 Cor. 11:23-29.)

2. How can we give till it hurts? (See Matt. 14:13-21.)

3. What is God personally calling you to give up or be willing to sacrifice until it hurts?

"Give me neither poverty or riches but give me only my daily bread. Otherwise I may have too much and disown you and say "Who is the Lord?" or I may become poor and steal, and so dishonor the name of my God."
—Proverbs 30:8b-9

CHAPTER 5

ABSENCE OF POSSESSIONS = CLOSENESS TO GOD

Have you ever considered the time you spend researching, shopping, accumulating, using, fixing, and finally discarding your possessions? Yet amazingly we do not have time for our families or serving others, and of course we lack the proper time we should be spending with God. We have already talked about the enormity of materialism and the raging battle it has created here in America. But what can we do about our personal battle as we deal with the constant desires to obtain possessions?

Have you ever tried to eliminate your possessions? This is exactly what happened to my husband and me when we spent a year in Mongolia. We each took the barest of essentials. We were required to live on a small stipend (though it was much greater than the income of the locals we lived among in our community). To understand this, think of each thing you believe you need every day—we probably went without it. No cell phones, no video games, inconsistent Internet access, no English television, very few books, very few store options, limited activities, and of course being stuck inside during extreme winter conditions, which lasted for a good portion of the time we were there. What did that mean for us Americans? For us, it meant a time of closeness with God.

Have you ever wondered how it was possible to follow God's direction to "be still and know that I am God" (Ps. 46:10)? Some of us may have experienced this in the middle of the night when everyone is asleep or when traveling to a remote island or a mountaintop all alone. While we were in Mongolia, we had many moments to be still and know that He is God, whether inside the house in the dead of the winter or wandering up the mountain just behind our home. We will always cherish those moments and even hours that were suddenly upon us as we no longer had all those "required possessions" stripping us of all we could be doing when we are here in America.

I remember repeatedly seeing my husband reading the New Testament that year, and he isn't even a reader. We were able to keep a running tab of our prayer requests and frequent answers to prayer. Because of the time we had, we were able to share in detail what God was doing in our lives and the lives of those around us. We also were able to discuss and spend quality time praying, especially for those He had called us to minister to while there. Unfortunately I cannot remember the last time I was able here in America to spend so much quality time with God. It is not that I have lost interest. I still do many things for God and in His name. However, I still find myself consumed by numerous earthly things. This is something I have to face and deal with on a daily basis.

In Mongolia, without all our stuff, our extended families, proper medical care, McDonald's, or many other things which you might think we cannot live without, we were able to depend on Jesus alone—the way He always meant things to be for His children. The third chapter of Proverbs had it right. We had our daily bread, a roof over our head, clothes on our back, as well as a couple more comforts that kept us from being poor. But because we lacked "material goods" we were able to depend on God rather than things.

All of this happened a few years ago. Since then, we struggle daily to go against the grain of society. We try to find a semblance to the closeness in our relationship with Christ that we experienced then. Now we sometimes have to wait until the middle of the night or the wee hours of the morning. For you to do this, it may take pulling the plug on the television or the computer, or maybe even putting away the toys (whatever is distracting us day after day). The more we can eliminate the easier it becomes. At times, whatever is set aside temporarily may need to become permanently eliminated if it causes us constant struggle.

Sometimes I wish I was back in Mongolia so I would not have all the distractions that seem to keep me from relying on God more quickly. I often find myself relying on media, doctors, friends, and other resources first. Most of us, however, will not spend a majority of our lives in a small Mongolian town. We have to figure out a way to draw closer to God that works for us and our families. We should start this process when our children are young. As most of us know, it is hard to teach old dogs new tricks. Letting go can be both painful and difficult at times, but the positive and eternal rewards are overwhelming and worth it.

Who among us would give anything to be in the situation of Adam and Eve and experience the closeness to God that they had available to them day in and day out? They had the opportunity to both walk with and talk to

God in a way we will never know on this side of eternity. However, we can give more of ourselves to Him rather than to the "things" around us, in order to begin a relationship of sweet communion with Him.

Take some time to evaluate your current situation. Can you easily identify some things that waste your time and are drawing you further and further away from God? Now is the time to eliminate or even escape from some of these things for a time. Maybe, like me, you will finally have the opportunity to experience what it is like to "be still" and listen for what God wants from you. You might be surprised when you actually hear what He has to say.

STUDY QUESTIONS

1. How much time do you spend with "your things?" Do they control you or do you control them?

2. What exactly did God mean in saying, "Be still and know that I am God" (Ps. 46:10)? Have you ever experienced this?

3. How can you relate Proverbs 3:7-9 to your own life?

4. What can you eliminate to become closer to God on a daily basis?

"Honor the Lord with your wealth, with
the firstfruits of all your crops."
—Proverbs 3:9

CHAPTER 6

HOW TO GET STARTED

As a couple, my husband and I have adopted a lifestyle of giving. We found it was easy to give when we were living in plenty. A few years ago we found ourselves in just the opposite situation. We had depleted some assets, including most of our savings, to help fund our stay in Mongolia. We had recently adopted our two children from Russia, and I had become a stay-at-home mom to take care of our young children. Some would say it was time to stop giving. No way! The needs of others around us were greater than they had ever been. It was just our resources that had been stripped. We knew that God still wanted us to give.

During this time our church had asked us to make our faith promise pledge for a building project. We believed this project would serve to further God's kingdom, and we wanted to be a part of it. We made our faith promise, knowing it would be more than a stretch for us based on our situation. After we made a decision and followed through, God provided nothing less than a miracle in our lives by opening the floodgates. We were faithful and obedient, and He gave to us in return just as He said He would (see Mal. 3). His promise was indeed fulfilled in our life.

From that time on, we saw God provide money to pay off debts that, no doubt, would have taken years to pay. We had several opportunities to give that came to our attention. Over and over again He provided the money for us to help meet those needs. We would be the first to admit that we often had to resist the urge to go and splurge when we had extra resources available instead of to give.

Contrary to popular opinion, God is not a God of legalism. He does, however, call us to give and to do so cheerfully (see 2 Cor. 9:7). But how and where do we initiate this process?

Perhaps starting your giving at 10 percent is a huge stretch for you. This was the amount required of the Jews in the Old Testament, which included giving 10 percent of whatever they had (animals, crops). We might remember the Bible portraying the Jews as a stubborn and stiff-necked people who had a lot of growing up to do. Very few of them seemed to go above and beyond. Are we unlike them?

This issue of giving may be a growing process for us as well. A few of you may need to start out with 1 percent, maybe 2 percent of your income, which may be more than you are currently giving. Along the way, increase your giving and change anything in your lifestyle you can do without. Continue to give more and more. But once you reach 10 percent, do not stop. Be faithful and give to God as He gives to you.

As God continues to provide more, you will be called upon to provide for others. What will this look like for you? That is between you and God. Something we have done in our family is to give at least 10 percent to our local church. We give other money above and beyond to meet other needs. This includes the support of missionaries, nationals who are partaking in ministries overseas, local and international charities, other church projects—and the list goes on and on. I have included at the end of the book a list of opportunities for volunteering (Appendix F). Some of these agencies are in need of great monetary support as well.

Most of us never have money handed to us. We have to work for it. Regardless of whether you have a high-paying job or have a low income, this chapter is for you. There are ways in which to stretch your income and begin to become a lifetime giver. In the past several years, God has shown both my husband and me many ways to earn extra money as well as how to effectively save money on everyday living. We hope you can embrace some of these opportunities to stretch your income and incorporate giving in your life.

The first thing that we had to do was to evaluate our monetary situation and create a working budget (see sample in Appendix G). As previously stated, this should be a bare-bones budget. It should simply categorize everyday needs. Again, we only budgeted needs, not wants.

For most people, making a budget is not too difficult, but sticking to it is an entirely different matter. So what is the best way to handle this? Keep your budget effortless. Ours is so simple that I keep it in a very small composition notebook in my purse. You could put yours on an iPhone, computer, or whatever works best.

Our budget has all the categories of spending needs in our family divided out by months, with space to mark our expenditures. The key is to keep track of all the expenses as soon as you buy or spend money. Sometimes right when I get back into the car I will write down what I have just spent. On the busier days, I will gather all my receipts when I get home and mark them down for the day. If you keep up with them on a daily basis, it will not get too overwhelming. About halfway through each month I tabulate expenses to see if I am where I should be. If I am getting too close to or over the budget limit, I calm down in spending. Sometimes I wait till the following month to buy an item. It is such a simple process. However, it has worked very well for our family in keeping us under control. We no longer need to be afraid of how quickly things add up, even when they are cheap or on sale. We know we are where we need to be. You can too.

Next, you have to simplify your lifestyle. This may sound hard to you, but it wasn't so hard for us. Since we had lived overseas in primitive camping conditions, we realized we did not need as much as we had thought. We did have to cut the mentality of keeping up with the Joneses. Who are the Joneses anyway? Who decides what level we live on? A very simple *us* is the correct answer. I wish all of you could see the places we have seen and realize how extravagant we all live. This transformed way of thinking brought us as a couple to a point of cutting purchases (which we had already begun to do within our budget). We would only buy something when an item would break down or become severely worn.

Along with this we realized our need to downsize. We live in a large old farmhouse with a barn. Many things had come into our possession over the years because we had storage space. God began to lead us to avenues in which to sell and disperse many things, bringing us revenue we could not believe existed, with limited effort on our part. We simply had to get started and accomplish something.

In our effort to disperse and downsize, God brought us to the use of online selling. Yes, contrary to popular opinion, the Internet is useful for more than just social and educational purposes. Opportunities are available to you if you are only willing to utilize them. Gone are the days of the classifieds in the local newspaper. Yes, they still exist for those of us who struggle to change and continue to hold on to the past, as well as to the very small audience that actually reads them. In addition, departed are the days of listing fees if you are willing to use the online selling venues. Though not new to many of you, these include eBay, Craigslist, and Amazon. We discovered in our research that each one had its own advantages and drawbacks, but by learning the tricks of the trade we have been able to use each one with great success.

There are so many helpful tips I could share with you about both buying and selling with each of these three sites. To provide some tips, I have dedicated Appendixes C, D, and E to cover each of these sites. I would challenge you to read about each of them if you are interested in getting started with online selling.

Selling online has been our largest source of side income, but it is not the only way to make and save money. Another source of income or savings is recycling. Of course there are the usual methods, such as recycling pop cans. However, there are many other items that might be unsellable to regular individuals but have value to someone. Any metal can be sold for a price; some types bring in more than others. Check your local directory to see where recycling centers may be located near you. As with everything, be sure to price around. Some places pay more than others.

Something else you can recycle is clothing, by selling or buying it (or donating it). There are the obvious ways of going about this, such as garage sales or secondhand stores. But have you tried resale shops? Most towns have consignment stores or resale shops that sell clothing and sometimes other items and give a decent percentage of the sale to the one who donates the item. This is especially profitable with brand name items. What a great asset to anyone's clothing budget if you consider that the clothing you purchase will have a value on it after you are done using it. It is especially successful when one has young children who constantly outgrow everything, sometimes before something is worn out.

I try to keep my children's clothing in good repair, not only because they are wearing it but also with the resale value in mind. To do this I use wool detergent to keep the colors in the clothing; I wash mostly in cool water; and I usually line dry. Instead of dragging all the clothing to the clothesline (which is very difficult for busy people), I use drying racks next to my washing machine where I can have easy access. Line drying helps prevent shrinking so that clothes last longer, plus it saves the electricity to run the machine. I always keep stain removers and other such items on hand to use instantly as needed.

Do not forget to recruit your children in this endeavor. Remind them that earning, saving, and giving is a family effort. Let them learn right alongside of you in your reeducation process.

Another item you might consider for recycling is ink cartridges for your computer printer. Office stores, such as Staples, offer ink cartridge rewards to be used like money in their store. Currently they offer two dollars for each cartridge turned in, up to ten cartridges each month. That is twenty dollars a month and two hundred forty dollars a year. We collect used cartridges all the time, sometimes even finding them at yard sales. This allows us to have a large in-store discount each month, which we in turn use on new ink cartridges for our own personal printer. With the rising cost of ink, what a great help this has become.

So maybe you are not into this recycling plan. Perhaps you do not have much to clean out. Have you tried couponing? Though it does not generate tangible dollar bills, it can save you dollars so you can use them for something else. Each week I sit down with a local newspaper to scour all the mainline grocery store ads.

Although you may think it is more practical to do all your shopping at one grocery store, it is not at all cost efficient. I personally have learned that in order to save the most money on food, I have to make my rounds of the stores. Over time I have learned the different stores' prices on the products I frequently buy. Therefore, when something goes on sale, I know whether it is really a sale compared to the price a competitor store is offering. Then I begin my coupon planning.

Though certain stores are cheaper than others, they may not be if they do not participate in double coupon programs. I do not consider myself an extreme coupon person, but I have learned to utilize coupons. First, I check the store sales on items I frequently buy. Then I search for any coupons I might have for those items. Those that have a match are usually the first items on my grocery list. They are not always our family's top choices or favorites. We sometimes have to do without our favorite things and go with the lowest cost item. Again, this is not about us. Often I get free or at least deeply reduced prices by shopping this way.

Currently the only reason we subscribe to our local paper is to get the weekly coupons. Most papers allow you to subscribe to only Sundays or a couple days of the week rather than buying it each day.

In addition to getting coupons in the local paper, I have also utilized online coupons. Two Websites I have found to be both reliable and useful for online coupons are coupons.com and smartsource.com. There are many others out there if you want to take the time to search. Some sites require you to register with them to receive periodic e-mail alerts. You can pick and choose.

Another option that I have also tried is buying manufacturer coupons that have already been clipped on eBay. This is especially useful when looking for a specific item that is usually more expensive. You can also find store-based coupons this way to save even more money.

Digital store coupons are also available by downloading the coupons into your cell phone. Some grocery stores participate in this.

Some stores allow you to use more than one coupon for a certain item. You can use your regular manufacturer's coupon in addition to the store coupon. Check your local grocery stores to see if they offer anything like this.

Also, if you forget to use your coupons when checking out, check to see if they can be redeemed at the service desk. I have done this both at Wal-Mart and at another grocery store. You simply produce the receipt showing you bought the item and you will receive the cash value on the coupon for that item.

Matching prices is another option for us money savers. So how does this work? Pick a store, such as Wal-Mart, that offers matching prices. Simply take in your ad for a competitor and they will give you the same price, no questions asked. This saves you from going to all the smaller grocery stores, drugstores, etc., while still getting their great weekly deals. Other stores, such as Lowes, also match ads. Don't be afraid to take the time and ask for these discounts. It is policy for these stores to give it. Again, do not forget that everything you have is the Lord's. Any extra money you acquire or save will ultimately go back to furthering His kingdom by you doing your part, if you are being faithful with your resources.

Something else you might do is to consider buying generic rather than brand name items when it comes to food and medication. As a social studies teacher I have had the opportunity to teach economics over the years. As part of my class, I would have the students do a "taste test." Each of the students would try the brand name and generic item, though they were not marked as such. Then they were to indicate which one tasted better. Although there were a few exceptions, most of them could not taste the difference, and in a couple instances they thought the generic item was actually better. What can we conclude from this? Most of us have been indoctrinated to believe brand names are always the best, and that in the case of medication only the brand-name item will really work. Again, only in a few instances is this actually true.

Sometimes our dedication to brand-name products becomes an issue of mental outlook. My mom recently reminded me how she used to buy generic Cheerios and put them in the real Cheerios box, because we liked to eat them out of the real Cheerios box as children. She did that with other items as well. Often we find ourselves laughing about such things as adults, but we can be nearly as bad ourselves when it comes to certain brand names.

When it comes to medication, I would highly suggest buying all your vitamins and miscellaneous household medicines at Sam's Club. They sell things in larger quantities at a fraction of the price you will find at Wal-Mart or any drugstore. I have shopped at store after store and found this to be true. Sometimes I am able to share some of my bulk medication with family members or friends and it is still cheaper than buying something at another store or buying brand name items. Another way to buy less expensive vitamins and supplements is to purchase them online. You will have to do your homework based on your needs to see which works best for you and your family.

Always, always, always, make a shopping list before you shop. As a general rule of thumb, put only what you need on your list, and stick to buying only what is on the list. You will be tempted to buy other things and get some "great deals." But often those great deals are actually items you do not need or even use. Many of those great deals will later become "great regrets."

Do not be afraid to take things back. Most grocery stores will give your money back or at least exchange the item for an equal item. Do not be afraid to take purchases back if you did not get what you paid for. I have taken back rotten produce or sour milk many times. Other stores can look up your items if they were purchased by credit card in their system, even if you do not have a receipt. There is no sense in discarding something that can be returned in exchange for something else.

Online purchases can be returned as well. Keep in mind you may have to pay the return shipping fee. This is still better than paying for an item you have no use for. However, it may cause you to more carefully make your purchases online, especially from less than reputable companies. Seek out companies that offer free shipping. Then if you are not satisfied, you are not paying shipping two times.

In the next chapters, I will share some other valuable tips to help you and your family save and stretch your dollars.

STUDY QUESTIONS

1. Is it possible to give something and also have it be given back to you? (See Luke 6:38.)

2. What is Psalm 37:4 referring to as it relates to this chapter?

3. According to 2 Corinthians 9:7, what kind of givers should we be?

4. What kind of giver are you? Why?

5. Is it necessary to create and live on a budget even if you have plenty of money?

6. What are the benefits of simplifying your lifestyle?

"Freely you have received, freely give."
—Matthew 10:8

CHAPTER 7

SIMPLIFYING RECREATION AND SOCIALIZING

We are living in a society that has become more and more busy and much more complex than ever before in history. With this in mind, most of us are seeking simple solutions to our ongoing problems. It is no different when dealing with money. Over time we all have found a few ways to make our lives easier. Let me share a few that I have discovered and we as a family have implemented within our household—time and time again—to save us money as we travel, recreate, and celebrate.

One of the areas where we have learned how to make cuts and save money is on vacations. Vacations, contrary to popular demand here in America, are not necessary. They are clearly a desire, not a need, though research has shown some rest and relaxation helps people to be more productive in their work.

Since vacations are a want and not a need, we never put them in our budget. In our house, vacations only happen when excess money is available (as from selling things). This is only after considering what other needs are more important. Even then, we try to make our vacations as economical as we possibly can.

As is generally known, the most expensive aspects of a vacation are transportation and lodging. These are the two areas in which we have been able to cut costs considerably. While there is not much we can do about the price of gas, we have other options to help us out.

Consider your vehicle. If it is older and less than reliable, you may want to think about renting a car. Out-of-town repairs may cost more than a rental and may cause you to get a rental anyway. When mechanics know you are traveling, you usually will not get a good price for your repair. Believe it or not (with very few exceptions), many people are out to make a quick buck. Weary travelers with broken-down vehicles are great candidates. Thus, if you are taking your own vehicle, make sure it is in tip top shape, to allow for the least amount of problems possible.

For car rentals, search the Internet for the best option. Use sites like priceline.com.

When you are picking up your rental car, they usually will advise you that they can fill the car's tank back up with gas when you return it, for a specific price per gallon, which will be listed for your viewing. Keep in mind that this price is usually higher than what the going rate is locally.

When we travel by car, we always try to take as much food with us as we can, especially so we can avoid convenience store prices. I usually pack a case or two of water, drink boxes for the kids, fruits, and other snacks. Additionally, this is no doubt the healthier way to go. Everyone knows that diets change on trips. This keeps us closer to our routine foods. This also limits our need to buy things upon reaching our destination. Some locations have higher prices than others, even at discount grocery stores. Bringing food from home will always save you a bundle.

Traveling by air can be fun but usually is more expensive. It all depends on the distance and time you have available. In our family we have utilized frequent flier mile programs, especially from our previous years of overseas travel, as well as credit card points. The latter is not recommended if your finances are not yet in control. For us, the lion's share of everything we spend in a month goes on our credit card. We make it a practice to pay everything off each month. This is never a problem if we are sticking to our budget. Over time we have accumulated a great deal of points and have used them to receive free airline tickets.

The great thing about the credit card points is the flexibility of us being able to use any airline at any time and be fully credited for whatever increment has been earned. Specific airline mileage programs have blackout dates in which travel is not allowed. However, they usually allow a set amount of miles to be used for travel to a variety of destinations (for example, anywhere in the continental United States). Credit card points, in comparison, are used on a dollar to dollar basis: If a ticket is $350, I will get covered for $350. When using frequent flier miles, however, I can go to a smaller airport in the United States that costs $550 and I will use the same amount of miles as for the $350 destination. Make sure to do your homework when utilizing these programs. There are loopholes, and you need to know what they are to save the most you can.

In some airline mileage programs, the miles will expire after a while if you don't maintain a certain level of activity with the airline. Make sure you know what your particular program requires for you to maintain active status. Even if your airline company has an expiration date if there is no airline activity, there are alternative ways to have account activity. For an example, United Airlines is a company that causes frequent flier miles to expire in the absence of account activity. However, you can sign up for a United Airlines credit card and receive points that keep your account active; hotel stays can do the same through such programs as Marriot Rewards. The use of the United Airlines credit card and Marriot Rewards through hotel stays only needs to be minimal to maintain the account activity.

When traveling by air, keep in mind the baggage fees most airlines are now charging. Travel as light as you can and utilize the maximum carry-on baggage allotment. In choosing what to pack, always consider where you are going and what it might cost to buy certain necessary items when you get there. If you are traveling with children, they too are allotted carry-on baggage. Be sure to use theirs before paying for baggage fees.

Another helpful tip concerns car seats. Some of us may not be aware that airlines allow one car seat per child, free of charge. If you do not bring one and plan on using a rental car company's car seats, be prepared for a price gouge. You can often go out and buy a new car seat for the cost of renting one. Again, rental car companies know you are in a bind when you land somewhere and do not have a car seat.

Often when we contemplate where to go on a vacation, we consider going to areas where we have friends and family nearby. It provides us an opportunity to see them again and, perhaps, gives us a place to stay. However, we limit our stay at any one place so as not to overwhelm or disrupt their family for any length of time. We have found one to two nights to be a good rule of thumb. For the remainder of the trip we stay in hotels. Our family usually stays within the same hotel chain as often as we can. Most hotel chains also have point systems where points can be accumulated and used for free lodging. When you sign up to become a member they will also make you aware of other promotional offers. We have had as many as five free or deeply discounted nights on one trip. When reserving your hotel room you will need to tell them your rewards number. They will not always remind you.

Another idea we have implemented when traveling is giving our children spending money they can use on the trip. I know that some families are spenders and have very few limitations when it comes to souvenirs and the like. As a family, we take a month or so before our trip and allow our children to earn extra spending money for the trip. Whatever they have earned by the time of the trip becomes their spending money. Of course my husband and I take care of the basics (food, lodging, transportation, entrance fees). This can be modified to match the age and situation of your children. This method allows our children to know exactly what they have. Since they earned it themselves, it is more special to them as well. This also makes the preparation time leading up to our trip more successful. Do not make just the destination of your trip all the fun, but include the preparation and the return home as equally exciting parts of the experience.

Most of us do not need to and should not go on extravagant vacations every year. You can have just as much fun traveling to places near home. Weekend getaways, camping trips, and even going to Grandma's house can become exciting if you make it that way.

Also, look in your local newspapers to see what is going on in your community. Many times there are free festivals, parades, concerts, and picnics. Consider going on outings where children's tickets are often free of charge. Go to parks or even take a walk in the woods. Sometimes a trip to the backyard to play a game with your children is easier, cheaper, and more fun than a vacation.

One other idea we have incorporated is birthday trips rather than birthday parties. We keep this as a family only event. The location is always a surprise to the children, which makes it even more exciting. Our destinations are usually places we deem to be too expensive for everyday entertainment. However, it works out well as two for the price of one: a birthday party and a trip in one great package.

If you do decide to go on a trip with expense, stick to your budget. Whatever you have allotted for the trip is what you should spend. Sometimes unexpected expenses arise, but generally overspending is our choice, and we can choose to control it. Again, forget where your neighbors and friends went on vacation. There is no way you will be able to keep up with everyone. Maybe it is time to stop trying and let God take over this area of your finances as well.

SUGGESTION

Host a small group to share any helpful tips each of you have learned over the years for earning or saving money for your family's recreation or for giving money away.

"Do not store up for yourselves treasures on earth, where moths
and vermin destroy, and where thieves break in and steal. But
store up for yourselves treasures in heaven, where moths and vermin
do not destroy, and where thieves do not break in and steal."
—Matthew 6:19

CHAPTER 8

PRACTICAL SUGGESTIONS FOR DAILY LIVING

Where do most of us spend the majority of our time? Hopefully the answer is our homes. This brings us to the next area where we can modify our practices and save the most money that we possibly can: simplifying our home life and limiting expenditures on our personal interests.

What we purchase and bring into our home and how we organize and store it can create challenges. Contrary to what you may think, buying supplies in bulk is not necessarily saving you anything. Most hoarders I know cannot find the items they bought a while back. They did it to save money by stocking up while the item was on sale. Yes, it can be beneficial and definitely less expensive to buy things ahead to save you money. But as with everything, this should be in moderation.

Alongside of simplifying your household is your need to be organized. Those who are more organized usually waste less regarding money and goods. Simplifying and organizing go hand and hand. "Everything has a place and everything in its place" is definitely a good motto to live by. When you are not organized, you often buy something you already have.

On the other hand, take advantage of those seasonal sales. Buy only what you will need till that same sale rolls around again next year. Also, in post-season sales I always purchase a variety of back-to-school items, Christmas and valentine cards, holiday candy, and the like at greatly reduced prices. However, I have selected areas in my home where I store these extra items. I don't buy more than what will fit in these designated storage areas. When things are really cheap, it is hard for some of us to say no. You may need to establish similar boundaries for yourself so you do not become or remain a hoarder.

Most of us grew up hearing the ever-so-popular phrases "turn off the lights" and "shut the door." At the time we thought Mom and Dad were just looking for another excuse to yell or nag at us. Now that we have become parents or live on our own, we find ourselves saying or thinking the very same things. The tables have turned and we are now the ones paying the bills—yes, those dreaded bills we receive each and every month. No matter what goes on in our lives and in the world around us, the bills still keep coming.

We cannot control the cost per watt used or the price we have to pay for a gallon of gas, but we can modify our use and cut out our personal charges. So yes, please turn off the lights when you leave the room, and please shut the door so the heat stays in the house. There are several other tips you can use to cut your utility costs. You could try using compact florescent light bulbs. They use 75 percent less energy and last eight to ten times longer. If you shop around you can sometimes find them just as cheap as incandescent light bulbs. Try limiting the use of your dryer. Line dry— especially clothing that is more likely to shrink. If you have a dishwasher, open it when it goes into the drying cycle. Let the dishes air dry the old fashioned way. Plan to have your family spend their evenings in one or two rooms in the house instead of lighting several. When possible, go to bed early! You will be putting dollars back into your pocket.

What else can you do? Have you tried cutting your cable plan? Is it possible that you could make better use of your money and your time? Limit the use of the television in general. Find something more productive and constructive for your family to do.

What about your cell phones? Though they are very useful in today's society, are you being the most efficient you can be while utilizing them? Are you part of a family plan for phones? Have you thought about maximizing the allotment on the family plan? It will save on each phone in the bundle. The more individuals on the family plan, the cheaper each phone becomes. This might also be the time to evaluate whether your child or teen needs their own phone. They do not need to have a phone just because their peers do. Make sure they are very responsible and that it is absolutely necessary. Most of us from the past generation or two lived without them when we were young, and we survived. You might also want to consider cutting off your landline. Most families rarely use them anymore.

We have already discussed keeping up with the Joneses. But if you truly need something repaired or upgraded, have you considered fixing it yourself? Everyone knows how expensive labor has become for just about any fix-it situation. In our home we do more than 75 percent of all projects and upgrades ourselves. Only the most difficult jobs are hired out. Not only that, but once we learn how to do a certain job, we can use that ability to benefit someone else who has a similar need.

Make sure to keep everything well maintained so you are able to get the maximum use out of it. Just because something has a ten-year warranty does not mean you have to throw it out after ten years.

What about gardening, landscaping, and mowing? Are you paying someone to do any of these things when you could be doing it yourselves? If you decide to hire someone for a task, have you considered hiring a person in need, such as one who has suddenly become unemployed, rather than paying a top rate to a high-priced company that might do a better job? This opportunity might give this unemployed individual a chance to remain productive and useful. You will also feel good about yourself for making this opportunity possible.

Have you ever considered how much money you spend on pets? If a survey was taken, we would probably find most homes have one or two pets. Personal incomes may vary from home to home, but even people on the poverty level often have pets. I have known people who struggled to pay their bills and sometimes even wondered where their next meal might come from, and yet they had a pet or two. Then there are those who yearly spend hundreds, even thousands of dollars, to have the best food, re-filtered water, teeth and fur care, and the like for their pets. Have you noticed the recent booming business of dog hotels and training centers? It may be worth considering and carefully weighing all the costs, time, and management it will take to care for that pet before following through with the desire to get one.

Having a pet is not a sin. Our family even has a couple cats. There are legitimate needs to have pets: for blind persons, the elderly, for therapy, and sometimes just for fun. But we can cross the line with this just as we can in any other area of our lives. As with everything we have previously discussed, this should be in moderation. You need to be willing to ask the following questions: Do you really have the money in your budget to care for a pet? Are you currently spending more each month on your pet or pets than people in other countries earn to provide for an entire family for the same period? Do you treat your pets as well as you treat your own children?

Some of us have become victims in this area. We have been sucked in by the media, neighbors, and friends to believe what we should do when it comes to pets instead of seeking God's counsel. After all, we live in a country that has a whole store aisle dedicated to "pet supplies." Thus we buy into the great desire in our culture to have a pet and consider it our job to provide for that need.

There are those who would argue that if one is not a "pet lover" then one would not understand the need to have a pet or to spend money on a pet. This may be true to a certain degree. However, this does not discount the true issue. Some of us have lost control in this area as well as in many other areas of our lives.

We need to revisit the term stewardship. Taking care of God's creation and having dominion over them includes animals. But if pets or animals have become the focus of much of our time, energy, and resources, we have probably crossed the line God has set for us as the stewards He wants us to be.

Finally, perhaps the greatest monetary consumption in our lives occurs with our hobbies and personal interests. If we are truly honest with ourselves, most of us would have to admit we have a hobby or two. Having a hobby can be fun, and sometimes it can be an opportunity to share with others. Maybe it is something you enjoy doing with your child, your spouse, or even a close friend. Perhaps it has even offered you possibilities you would not previously have known existed. However, this is yet another area of your life you will need to hold in check if you are to become the steward God has called you to become.

As with everything else, money and time spent on the hobbies will need to be budgeted. Even if your budget can afford a larger, more expensive item for your hobby or interest, you should ask yourself these questions:

- What is my purpose in having this item?
- Am I willing to share it with others, or is it only for me alone?
- Can I justify the time spent to get my money's worth out of it?
- Is God calling me to do something else with the money and I am simply resisting that?
- What am I teaching my children through my purchase, if I hope to help them understand the concept of stewardship? Are they seeing consistency in all other areas of my life but failure when it comes to hobbies and the time and money I spend on them?

For most of us, giving will only take place by withholding something we may really desire and enjoy (perhaps making a true personal sacrifice). Perhaps it is our hobby. Some of you may argue your hobby or personal interest is not really that expensive. Are you sure? Have you kept track of how much you spend on video games, fishing gear, garage sale items, art materials, baking, or scrapbooking, not to mention things like motorbikes and boats? From my own observation, I would venture to guess we spend much more than we realize on hobbies.

These are just a few areas in which we have effectively cut costs in our household. You may have a few others. Do not merely read this or think of your own ideas. Act on them. Challenge yourself to start changing the way you conduct your everyday life. Are you being the good steward that God wants you to be in these areas of your life? Only you can answer that question.

STUDY QUESTIONS

1. Are you accumulating earthly possessions?

2. What does the Bible teach us about accumulating earthly possessions? (See Matt. 6:19-20.)

"So do not worry, saying, 'What shall we eat?' or 'What shall we drink?' or 'What shall we wear?' For the pagans run after all these things, and your Heavenly Father knows you need them. But seek first His kingdom, and His righteousness, and all these things will be given to you as well."
—Matthew 6:31-33

CHAPTER 9

EVALUATING YOUR PRIORITIES

We have discussed several different areas in which we can save money at home, while on vacation, and in other contexts. How about a few more?

What about your family's vehicle? First you need to evaluate your situation. Areas you should consider include the size of your family, your job needs, and of course your family's budget. How much should you actually allot for a car within your budget? Whatever that number may be, stick to it! Do not be swayed by what others around you have. Many of them are in debt and do not have the first idea of the concept of giving and stewardship. You might become their best example. Very few people can truly afford a brand new car paid in full. So what do your options include?

For many of us, this may be used cars. Some can pay for the used car in full with the sale of their current car and some savings. For others the option may be a new car with quite a steep payback plan. Again, as a proponent of stewardship (which I hope you are becoming as well), there is probably no way to justify an $80,000 vehicle no matter what your status may be. Think simple and useful. Consider limiting the unnecessary options you know you can live without. If you get paid mileage and travel extensively for your job, you may need a very reliable car, and perhaps this justifies a brand new one. If you live five to ten minutes from your work place with a very moderate income, a good used car should be satisfactory. Again, decide what your budget can afford, not the lifestyle you wish you had.

If you do decide to buy a brand new car, make sure you do your homework so you are aware of the different promotional plans the car companies offer. We have participated in a promotional that allows us a three-year period to pay back our loan with no interest. We always put some money down so we are able to handle the monthly payments. If something happens to decrease our income, we can simply sell the car for more than we owe on it and buy a decent used car. There is something else to be aware of if you make payments this way. Once you get closer to finishing your payments, the loan company will tell you your payments are now less. Just continue to pay the same amount in order to pay it off during that three-year window. In addition to this, we always allot a certain amount of money for a car payment each month. If we have already paid off our car loan, we put away that same amount of money each month. When we go to buy a new car, we then have a reasonable amount of money for a down payment on the car.

When getting a new car, carefully consider what to do with your old one. Many people prefer to trade in their used vehicles to avoid the headache of selling them, and it gives them some cash to use toward the purchase of a new one. While this may be easier, most of the time the trade-in offer is a fraction of the price you would get if you sold it on your own. To get the most for your money, you will likely want to sell your car yourself. To preserve its value, make sure to treat your car with the best care while you own it. This is no different than taking care of your clothes or other personal things. Keep your car clean and in good repair. These are necessities that will appeal to future buyers. Such things are also the mark of good stewardship.

So what about shopping? We have already talked about shopping for groceries and supplies. What about shopping for everything else? As to clothing, I have already provided a couple suggestions; here are a few more. This is one area in which most of us in America have been overtaken. Just look into one of your closets in your home and the argument would be closed. Even those with more limited incomes have more than enough clothes. Yes, we all know that our culture requires certain things from us, especially the quality of our appearance. It can be expected with certain positions. But even then, do we really need all we have and how much we continue to accumulate in this area of our lives? That is only the first problem.

Another aspect may be greed. How about the money we spend to accumulate all these articles of clothing? Those of us who live in climates that vary throughout the year may be able to support a claim of needing more than others to accommodate all the seasons. However, if we are really truthful with ourselves, we might admit we have become greedy when it comes to apparel. We would not be caught dead wearing the same article of clothing more than twice a month. Truly there is nothing wrong with looking nice, as long as you are living within your means and are being a steward of what God has entrusted to you.

When it comes to buying clothes you really do need, make sure you budget what you can afford and stick to the budget. For those of us on a very strict budget, choices may be limited. For others with more resources, it may be time to rethink this area. This might be an area where we could cut back to have more money to pay off our debts and ultimately give to God what is His.

Let's start with used clothing. Some have relatives and friends that give hand-me-downs. Always take everything you are given. In spite of how you feel, you can usually find something you can use. Remember why you are doing this. Next, check out garage sales. You can usually find things for a fraction of the original value. Many times things are worn out, but if you look enough you will find some good items and even some new ones. I personally try to look for brand name items still in good repair. Those I can't personally use I send to my local resale shop on consignment. This way I can usually get back the money I paid for the item. So far I am at the level of spending little or no money from my clothing budget.

Occasionally I will visit consignment shops and other secondhand stores. These stores, however, tend to be overpriced for often-worn items that could be found at garage sales for much less. Only if I find brand name items in great repair will I consider buying from secondhand stores.

Once I have exhausted my "used" option I head to brand new clothing stores. It is my observation over the years that quality is better than quantity when it comes to clothing. Sometimes I am better off buying something slightly more expensive that will last longer. Unlike some people, I rarely frequent the regular malls. Unless I can find seasonal sales or specials, the prices are simply astronomical. When you shop around at other places you can often find brand new articles of clothing for used store prices. The best prices I have found are at outlet malls during the end of each season of the year. I have to keep myself in check, because

I often find such good deals that I could buy more than I actually need. At least I know these brand name clothes are great sellers at the resale shop. Plus my family can look good without spending so much money. Occasionally I shop at other stores, again at the end of each season to get the deepest discounts. Spending full price on clothing is usually reserved for rare situations.

Something else I have done with children's clothing is buying ahead at least one to two sizes. Styles do not change that radically in one or two years, but costs can. Again, it is about being smart, not popular. I do this more with certain items that can be tremendously expensive when not on sale. Shoes, jeans, and dresses are just a few of these items. I have them organized by future sizes and seasons in closets and drawers so that they are easy to find when we are ready to use them. Of course I still use in-store coupons and shop special sales when I get the opportunity. With this method I am usually at or below our monthly clothing budget. This gives me extra money to do something else.

Another area of spending for most families is on schooling and extracurricular activities. All of us have our own preferences and opinions on this topic. I am not here to tell you what God wants you and your family to do. However, there are some helpful suggestions about what I have observed and learned in this area as well.

There are many areas where we can save money. But who can put a price tag on our children? You will have to prayerfully consider what God would have you do, whether choosing public school, a Christian or other private school, or homeschooling. Each has its own advantages and disadvantages that you as parents will have to consider. Some of us choose homeschooling, because we feel it is our responsibility alone to educate our children. If you have the means, the knowledge, and the patience, this can be a grand opportunity for you and your children. It can be a great alternative to public schooling for those who are on a tight budget. However, if you feel public schooling is not for you and your children and God is calling you to put your children in a Christian school, He can provide for that as well. Such as been the case for us.

We had started out with homeschooling, partly due to the cost of Christian education and not being fully happy with the public school option. For various reasons we started by putting our oldest child in a Christian school, with some anxiety about what it would cost. Instead, we saw God provide, and we didn't even miss the money that we paid in tuition. Even after that we still had money to give. Then a year later we took a deeper plunge and put our second child in the Christian school. Again we saw God provide, with not much of a change in our lifestyle. Now that both our children are in school, I am free to work some. But instead of needing that money for tuition, we are able to have more money to give. My point is that God will provide the money you need if He is calling you to do something.

What about the extracurricular schedule you have for your children? How much of your time, money, and energy is drained by this? I know people who have their children in sports, music lessons, and other activities year round. Adding up the cost of the activity fees, lessons, extra transportation, and eating on the run (fast food), it seems these families could have easily paid for a Christian school education instead. Once again we are reminded that it is all about our choices. Perhaps it is time to reflect and decide if your choices about your time and money are God honoring. Are you being a good steward with your children as they watch your example in this area of living?

For those of you who do choose Christian education, there may be some additional helps you may not be aware of. Mileage reimbursement from the state is available from the site of your local school district to the Christian or private school your child attends. This may vary from state to state. Here in Ohio where I reside, we send a request to our local school district in the fall of each school year. They send us an approval letter with a paper to sign. We receive whatever money is allotted for that school year the following June. Though it is not a lot of money, what a great help it has been with the transportation costs of getting to and from school. Some Christian schools have enough students from the same district to warrant the use of the district's bus to the school. Again, most of us are paying taxes for our local school district—why not find a way for a fraction of that tax money to be used specifically for your children's benefit? You can also try carpooling to save on the cost of gas and vehicle usage.

Here are some other ideas to help make it possible to attend a Christian or private school. One is for a parent to volunteer at the school. Sometimes there is a tuition reduction for putting in hours at the school. Also, for those of you who are not familiar with it: Christian schools provide discounts for second, third, fourth, or additional children. Occasionally these schools even offer scholarships. These are all things you need to check out if God is calling you to this type of education for your children.

There are other alternatives to the time, energy, and money many of us spend on schooling and extracurricular activities. Do you have a talent? Does another parent you know have a talent? You can both teach each other's children free of charge. Have you tried to look for less expensive and less time-consuming sports alternatives? Our church recently began an Upward basketball/cheerleading league for our county. It is fairly inexpensive, and the time required for practices and games is minimal. Maybe one of these leagues can be found in your area and offers other varieties of sports.

Again, search, search, search, and do not settle for what everyone else is doing. God expects more from us who are His good stewards.

STUDY QUESTIONS

1. What does Matthew 6:31–33 teach us?

2. Have you considered what you have, what you make, and what you need? What is God calling you to do in each of these areas?

3. Evaluate your priorities and choices. Are you doing things the way God has called you to do them?

"For where your treasure is, there your heart will be also."

—Luke 12:34

A WHOLE NEW TRAIN OF THOUGHT

Everyone has heard the phrase, "I lost my train of thought." When it comes to managing our finances and learning how to give, a whole new train of thought is exactly what we need. Regardless of whether we are willing to admit it, we are all programmed a certain way. Contributing factors include the way we were raised, our surrounding environments, and our specific bent in education. Certain results can be expected. Thus it becomes difficult to retrain ourselves with a whole new way of thinking.

We live in a world in which the pursuance of possessions takes precedence over almost everything. This seeking after possessions places a division between us and God (see Luke 12:30). As one Bible commentary says, "When we are consumed with possessions, there can be little left in our hearts for God."[4] Yet Jesus taught time and time again to do the direct opposite. "Do not store up for yourselves treasures on earth," he said (Matt. 6:19). We should not

---

[4] Radmacher, Allen, and House, *Nelson's Compact Bible Commentary*, 721.

worry about our life and pursuing things, Jesus also said, since our Heavenly Father knows we need them and will provide them (see Luke 12:22). The letter to the Philippians states, "Do not be anxious about things" (Phil. 4:6). We are told to let the God who knows our needs be in charge rather than abandoning Him and running after our needs all on our own.

Now that we have been made aware of what the Bible teaches concerning material gain and its uses, it is time to act. Too often we pick up a book or article or we hear someone speak on a pertinent subject like this, and we think to ourselves, "Yes, this is relevant. It is so true. I really do have things to change which could make a difference in my life and in the lives of others around me." Yet the moment we shut what we are reading or leave a seminar or a church service, we quickly forget and go on our merry way. Life continues as usual, and nothing changes for anyone.

In this area of managing money and learning, many do absolutely nothing. Some of us even have good intentions. Yet good intentions flop after very little effort and trial. In this case, however, we are being disobedient to many of the commands God has given us. Thus we might ask ourselves, how do we know when the Scripture is giving us a command?

Perhaps it is time for an elementary grammar lesson. Most of us vaguely remember learning what action verbs are. They are words that indicate what a person or thing can do—something involving an action. As already noted several times throughout the previous chapters, we are able to discover what God has identified as some required actions: "be content;" "offer hospitality;" "command those who are rich;" "oversee orphans and widows;" "you give;" "sowing generously;" "freely give;" "give;" and "deny himself," just to name a few. Jesus demands us to actively be doing all these things mentioned here, and more. We are to be doers of the Word, not hearers only (James 1:22). Jesus even told His own disciples, when He was preparing to ascend and leave the earth, to "go and make disciples of all nations, baptizing them in the name of the Father, and of the Son, and of the Holy Spirit, and teaching them to obey everything I have commanded you" (Matt. 28:19-20a).

Most of us have much to learn and practice in order to obey all the commands the Bible has given us, especially in the area of giving. The key is being willing to be taught. Thank the Lord daily for giving you a lifetime to learn.

STUDY QUESTIONS:

1. What factors have contributed to your current view on money, possessions, giving, and serving?

2. What can possessions cause? (See Luke 12:30.)

3. What did Jesus teach us about possessions? (See Matt. 6:19; Luke 12:22; Phil. 4:6.)

4. What are some of the commands mentioned in the Bible in regard to giving and self-sacrifice? Are you actively pursuing the commands He has given all of us, including you?

GIVING AND SERVICE EVALUATION

If you are like me, you often spend time in self-evaluation. Since none of us will reach perfection until we are glorified, self-evaluation and accountability are not only important, but are required by God. You can refer to this test to gauge whether you are improving in this very important area of living: giving to and serving others. This exercise will show which areas need the most improvement. You will be able to rate yourself in each category and tabulate your score.

Rate yourself for each statement based on a range of 1-10, with 1 representing it is an area you struggle in and 10 representing that you are doing very well in that area. You may also choose to have someone else evaluate you and compare your results and theirs to see how others may view your lifestyle of giving and serving others.

Let's get started!

_____ 1. Stewardship (our accountability as managers of what God has provided for us here on earth).

_____ 2. Hard-working (not prone to laziness).

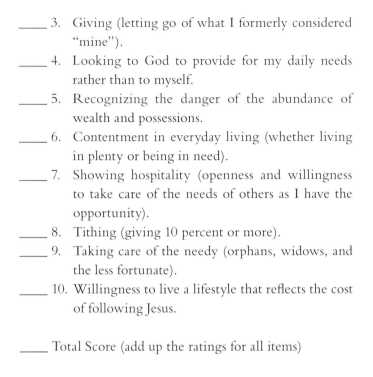

_____ 3. Giving (letting go of what I formerly considered "mine").

_____ 4. Looking to God to provide for my daily needs rather than to myself.

_____ 5. Recognizing the danger of the abundance of wealth and possessions.

_____ 6. Contentment in everyday living (whether living in plenty or being in need).

_____ 7. Showing hospitality (openness and willingness to take care of the needs of others as I have the opportunity).

_____ 8. Tithing (giving 10 percent or more).

_____ 9. Taking care of the needy (orphans, widows, and the less fortunate).

_____ 10. Willingness to live a lifestyle that reflects the cost of following Jesus.

_____ Total Score (add up the ratings for all items)

INTERPRETATION OF YOUR TOTAL SCORE

90-100: You are a self-sacrificing individual, willing to go above and beyond to reach for Christ-likeness.

80-90: You are well on your way in recognizing the needs of others and your part in meeting those needs.

70-80: Your eyes are opening to the area of giving and service, but you still have much to learn about letting go.

Below 70: You can take this test again in the future to check for improvement.

After personally taking this self-inventory test and scoring myself in each category, I found some areas in which I definitely need to improve. In spite of all the things God has taught me about self-sacrifice and stewardship, there is so much more to learn. May you also begin to learn as He reveals what He wants of each of us. Please review this Scripture once again:

"Command those who are rich in this present world not to be arrogant nor to put their hope in wealth, which is so uncertain, but to put their hope in God, who richly provides us everything for our enjoyment. Command them to do good to be rich in good deeds, and to be generous and willing to share. In this way they will lay up a treasure for themselves as a firm foundation for the coming age, so that they may take hold of the life that is truly life" (1 Tim. 6:17-19).

TOPICAL LIST OF BIBLE CITATIONS

STEWARDSHIP

Gen. 1:28b
Matt. 25:14-30
Luke 6:38
1 Tim. 6:17-19

GIVING

Deut. 8:11-20
Deut. 12:28
Ps. 37:16-27
Matt. 10:8
Matt. 14:13-21
Mark 12:41-44
Luke 6:38
2 Cor. 6:6-15
1 Tim. 6:17-19

Tithing

Deut. 14:28-29
Mal. 3:6-12

Taking Care of the Needy

Deut. 8:11-20
Deut. 12:28
Ps. 37:16-27
Matt. 6:3-4
Acts 6:1-7
1 Tim. 5:3-4
James 1:27

The Cost of Following Jesus

Matt. 6:19-21
Matt. 10:9-10a
Luke 9:58
Luke 12:31-33
Luke 14:27

Contentment

Prov. 30:7-9
Luke 12:22
Phil. 4:12b-13
1 Tim. 6:8-9

Danger of Wealth/Possessions

Prov. 15:16-17
Prov. 16:8; 19
Prov. 23:4
Prov. 30:7-9
Eccl. 5:10-12
Matt. 6:24
Luke 12:30
1 Tim. 6:17-19
2 Tim. 2:2
James 2

God's Provision for Us

Matt. 6:27
Luke 12:22

TIPS FOR SELLING ON EBAY

Over the past few years most of us have heard the buzz about the eBay Website. Many of you have even made purchases from this site. However, when you are downsizing in your home life, this is one great outlet for selling those unnecessary items you still have in your possession. Most of us avoid doing things such as selling items on eBay because we think we lack the time and that it is just too hard. In our digital age, shopping online is quickly overtaking traditional shopping. This is especially true when buying or selling vintage and specialty items (goodbye pawn shops). This brings us to the question of the hour: How do I get started?

Assuming you have already done some cleaning and collecting around the house and garage, start by searching for like items on eBay. See if anyone is buying anything that you are trying to sell. If so, what kind of price are people willing to pay? If your item is a hot seller, get your photo of the item loaded, read the site's instructions about how to list the item, and get it going. When you become more comfortable using eBay, make sure to take multiple photos at once of the many items you plan to sell at one at a time.

This way you will not waste time by downloading each individual picture.

Here are some other helpful hints when going through the listing process. For the length of the listing I would recommend seven days, depending on the quantity of like items for sale at that time. If there are thousands of items like yours, you may want to choose a shorter duration. It is also better to end listings in the evenings or on weekends when possible. Most people have much more time to search for items and make bids at these times. For starting prices, search for others selling the same or a similar item. Place your starting price at or slightly below theirs for a starting bid. It all depends on how quickly you want to move and sell the item. Always remember, the higher your item sells for, the higher your selling fee will be.

The eBay site offers free listings for those who are starting out. I have seen offers for fifty to one hundred free listings a month. Occasionally eBay has different promotional offers for more free listings for a designated period of time. My husband and I have found fifty listings a month is more than enough to keep us busy as a side hobby. Taking on more than this can be time consuming and stressful.

What kinds of things are worth being sold on eBay? The answer is just about anything. We have sold empty boxes, used parts for machinery, vintage items, toys and collectibles, clothing, instruments, car accessories, movies, and books. The list of possibilities is endless! Sometimes it is true what you hear: One person's junk just might be another person's treasure. Your closets, drawers, and garages might have valuables you never knew existed.

Some items are great money makers, while other items may sell for just a small profit. This all depends on your items and your motive for selling them. In our household, we are not out to get a fortune for ourselves. We are trying to generate some extra income to raise our level of giving and become the stewards God wants us to be.

There are some other helpful tips when selling on eBay. These are some of the things we as a couple learned the hard way; we would love to spare you the hassle. One is in the area of shipping.

There are multiple ways to ship your eBay items to the buyers. The simplest is the print and ship option. It is quick and easy—just a couple clicks and then printing a label. Saving pennies on shipping costs can make a difference, since some items you sell may not be worth as much and you will want to make the most you can. When shipping through eBay you will receive a tracking number for nineteen cents, otherwise you will be charged seventy-five cents when you obtain it at the post office. This is not including the savings on gas you would otherwise use driving to and from the post office, especially if the post office's location is not convenient. You can affix a label on a box and put it in your own mailbox. Larger mailing boxes can be purchased if this is ongoing. Also, most people are not aware that the Postal Service picks up packages at your home (or from a place on your property that you designate) when this is requested online for your local postal pickup. This must be requested the night before pickup.

Another alternative to using the eBay shipping service or driving to the post office is to use the Postal Service Website to print labels to ship. They offer a service called Click-N-Ship on their site. On this site you will find slightly reduced rates from what you would pay when going to the post office directly. It is easiest to ship by priority mail when using this site. Priority mail shipping boxes of all shapes and sizes can also be ordered online from this same site. These can be sent to you free of charge in bulk quantities at your request. We have found this to be a great option for shipping items sold through venues other than eBay.

Some other helpful tidbits for shipping items sold on eBay include getting the right weight and sizing information when listing your items. We discovered early on the importance of investing in a small scale that shows grams, ounces, and pounds. Make sure to enter the correct weight and measurements in order to determine the most accurate mailing rate. Guessing will cost you, because the buyer will be expected to pay only the shipping price you quoted, not what it actually costs you to ship it, even if that is higher. Also I strongly suggest choosing to calculate shipping based on the buyer's location rather than offering a flat rate to all buyers. Sending something to a neighboring state is much less expensive than sending something clear across the country. When listing our item's potential shipping cost, we always take into account what the item might cost to send to one of the furthest destinations.

Those of you who have not mailed things frequently may need some assistance on the different rates of mailing with the United States Postal Service. For most items, mailing rates are based on weight and dimensions. For items between one and thirteen ounces, the best rate for mailing is first class. For items between one and three pounds for which the destination is near, priority mail is often best. Items that are heavier (up to seventy pounds), but not necessarily large, can be put in flat rate priority mailing boxes for one flat fee. For all other mailings, especially when mailing heavy and larger size items, parcel post is often the best rate. For items heavier than seventy pounds, you may want to try other shipping companies such as UPS, FedEx, or DHL.

When large or heavy items will not sell well on eBay due to the cost of shipping, try Craigslist. On eBay, however, there is an option to avoid shipping by requiring the buyer to pick up the item.

As with anything, selling on eBay is a learning process. We as a couple are constantly discovering new tricks to make us better sellers. Sometimes you will sell things instantly, and other times you will have to lower your price over and over and then you will finally sell your item. Be patient! We have sold about 80-90 percent of the items we have ever listed. We have had such success that we have family members giving us items to sell. Instead of asking for profit, they have given us the liberty to give the proceeds to various needs.

Refuse any longer to put off starting. Our success can be yours too. If you follow some of these helpful tips and maybe a few that you learn along the way, you will make a profit, clean out your closet, and have extra money to give again and again.

TIPS FOR SELLING ON CRAIGSLIST

Craigslist is an online classifieds Website. It is divided according to region, with your greatest potential customer base in your own vicinity. Others outside your region, however, have the option to search other regions and still find your item. Compared to eBay, your customer base will be much smaller, based on the area in which you live.

What are the advantages of using Craigslist rather than eBay? One benefit you will find is that there are no fees involved that eat into your profit on the sale. Also, you can list things for long periods of time as opposed to the three, five, and seven days that eBay offers.

Based on a great deal of experience with Craigslist, I suggest relisting often. Although it is not required, relisting frequently will keep you on the top of the list for the type of items you are trying to sell. Craigslist displays items according to the day they were listed, with the most recent days shown first.

Include multiple pictures of your item. Pictures are not required but will be a valuable asset in selling your item.

Also remember, people are looking for a "great deal." For specialty items on which you would like to receive a higher profit, use eBay.

The Craigslist customer base is much more limited than eBay. Sometimes it will take a while to sell things, and you will have to list them again and again. Other times it will seem like you are selling things instantly. Much like our experience on eBay, we have sold about 80-90 percent of what we have listed on Craigslist.

For both eBay and Craigslist I would recommend keeping files of your sales. This enables you to keep track of the money you have made and to store the information safely. It will also allow you to have something to look back to if the need should arise in the future. Each of us will be held accountable to God for what we have, so good recordkeeping is important.

It is my hope you will soon have an opportunity to try Craigslist for selling the items you no longer need or want. You will be both excited and amazed when you start this process. Just remember why you are doing it, and God will help you generate money through this avenue.

TIPS FOR SELLING ON AMAZON

A mazon is another wonderful way to sell your products online. While eBay is predominantly an auction site, Amazon acts like a regular store. Buyers pay the price that is listed, in addition to the shipping. Everything listed is classified on a value system reflecting the condition of the item being sold. The item can be described as fair, good, like new, or new. Usually the items that are considered more used than new, but still are acceptable, will be marked as fair.

Amazon does not require any fees to list an item. Significantly, items can be left on Amazon for indefinite periods of time (month after month).

Keep in mind that you may want to update the price of the product you are trying to sell; otherwise, over time several people may lower their prices for similar items and sell their products long before you do.

If you are able, it is important to utilize the feedback mechanisms for buying and selling (something that also is done on eBay). As you make sales and buyers give feedback, this will give seller ratings by your name. The higher your ratings, the more likely you will get the first chance at selling your particular product or item. People are not as eager to buy items from those with lower ratings.

What should you sell on Amazon? Amazon works best for smaller, more popular items. I most often use it for selling books, DVDs, CDs, and other forms of media. These types of things can be shipped through the Postal Service as media mail, which greatly reduces the cost of shipping. Other items such as food, fabrics, and toys can also be sold on Amazon (or eBay). It will be your job to assess the costs involved and decide which avenue you should use to sell your particular item.

Keep in mind when selling on Amazon that there is a seller's fee that you will be responsible for. Do not put your price so low that you will be unable to cover your costs. I have done this in the past. If you are not going to make much money from selling your item, it will not be worth your valuable time. Some of this will be trial and error. However, I suggest you make at least a couple dollars for each item, or it will not be worth your time to sell that item. Also, remember that the cost of shipping continues to rise.

When trying to make the most you can while selling online, it helps to be fully prepared for the packing and shipping tasks. We have built a storage area within our home for items such as extra boxes, packing materials, and brown paper for wrapping. We always save any packing materials in decent enough shape to be reused. So far we have rarely had to restock these supplies, except packing tape. Again, use the free boxes offered for priority shipping on the Postal Service Website. The key is to always be organized. It will help you make more money, and you will not be stressed in the process.

Appendix F

❖

Suggestions for Volunteer Opportunities

Jesus has called us to love the unlovable. The ultimate example was Jesus Himself. He loved the world so much He gave up His own life for us unworthy sinners. The least we can do is follow in His steps and be willing to take on the nature of a servant to the unlovable (see Phil. 2:7). If the Good Samaritan could love someone who was hated by his people, we can do the same (see Luke 10:25-37).

The following are some suggestions about organizations or programs you may want to look into as you seek opportunities to be more like Christ. Each time I have heard testimonies from individuals, I have found that most people are saved by the sacrifice of people like you and me taking on the nature of a servant, showing our willingness to love those around us, and finally sharing with them the hope we have in Christ.

- disaster relief programs
- safe houses
- after school programs (youth, children)

- Habitat for Humanity
- Big Brothers; Big Sisters
- crisis pregnancy centers
- Child Evangelism Fellowship
- Youth for Christ
- soup kitchens
- rescue missions/homeless shelters
- Right to Life
- Adopt a Family
- food pantries
- carpooling those in need
- clothing swaps/COOP
- free garage sales
- foster care programs
- hosting exchange students
- food and clothing drives/distribution
- volunteering for the American Red Cross
- free babysitting
- providing scholarships for extracurricular activities for underprivileged children
- nursing homes
- prison fellowships
- working with new immigrants or second language speakers
- free English lessons
- providing free tutoring or music lessons
- community gardens
- numerous opportunities available through local churches

This list barely scratches the surface. If God is calling you to reach out and do something, He will lead you to the agency or the individuals He wants you to work with. Some of us will only ever be volunteers in existing organizations. God, however, may have given you the means to start and fund an organization to meet specific needs for any number of things either at home or across the world. May God give each of us desire, vision, and strength to listen to His leading in reaching out to those around us as well as to those across the globe.

SAMPLE BUDGET

(Monthly Expenditures)

January (1-1)
($3,200) monthly budget amount available

Gifts ($50)
$15.00 (1-6)
$5.00 (1-12)
$25.00 (1-21)

$45.00 (total)

Miscellaneous ($175)
$16.50 (1-3)
$30.00 (1-9)
$15.95 (1-11)
$3.50 (1-13)
$7.85 (1-16)
$19.99 (1-19)
$6.50 (1-22)
$7.95 (1-27)
$36.50 (1-30)

$144.74 (total)

Food ($400)
$30.00 (1-5)
$45.00 (1-8)
$63.00 (1-10)
$28.00 (1-14)
$40.50 (1-16)
$33.10 (1-19)
$50.15 (1-23)
$40.25 (1-25)
$28.70 (1-27)
$35.90 (1-30)

$394.60 (total)

Entertainment ($100)
$22.00 (1-1)
$15.60 (1-9)
$25.00 (1-15)
$10.05 (1-19)
$23.99 (1-25)

$96.64 (total)

Gas ($175)
$35.00 (1-4)
$28.00 (1-9)
$34.00 (1-15)
$45.00 (1-21)
$10.00 (1-28)
$15.50 (1-30)

$167.50

House Payment
$650.00
Insurance
$175.00

Medical ($175)
$25.00 (1-10)
$10.00 (1-13)
$25.00 (1-18)
$50.00 (1-27)

$110.00 (total)

Electric ($250)
$250.00
Fuel
$50.00
Phone
$55.00
Tithe
$320.00

Savings
(   )*

Clothing ($200)
$25.20 (1-3)
$35.99 (1-7)
$20.15 (1-10)
$15.99 (1-15)

$5.75 (1-22)
$50.25 (1-26)
$12.65 (1-29)

$165.98 (total)

Car Payment
$250.00

Childcare ($50)
$20.00 (1-12)
$25.00 (1-19)

$45.00 (total)

Home Upkeep ($50)
$15.55 (1-20)

$15.55 (total)

Auto Upkeep ($75)
$25.20 (1-12)
$15.00 (1-20)

$40.20 (total)

★Note: Each family will need to sit down and decide which areas necessary expenses need to be allocated. Each time there is an expense, mark down the amount and date to easily be able to tabulate monthly expenses in any particular category. (1-5) would indicate the first month, and the fifth day. In the categories where you do not use the total amount allocated, this becomes your savings for the future. As you make more money, you will be able to reserve more for a savings fund and more for giving to other needs.

January Total
$2,975.01 (total monthly expenses)
$224.79 (money remaining after monthly expenses is available for building your savings and giving to specific needs as God calls you)

Helpful Financial Resources

I highly recommended the following sources if you are seeking more specific information on managing your money. These ministries offer training courses and sessions to walk you through life-changing transitions and help you manage your money.

- Crown Financial Ministries; http://www.crown.org
- Dave Ramsey; http://www.daveramsey.com

Bibliography

Holy Bible, New International Version. Grand Rapids, MI: Zondervan.

Radmacher, Earl, Ron Allen, and H. Wayne House. *Nelson's Compact Bible Commentary.* Nashville, TN: Nelson Reference & Electronic, 2004.

Trent, Butler C. *Holman Bible Dictionary.* Broadman & Holman, 1991. http://www.studylight.org/dic/web/.

Webster, Noah. *Noah Webster' American Dictionary.* 1828.

About the Author

Sue Myers holds a master of ministry degree from Bethel College, Indiana, as well as taking classes at Grand Rapids Theological Seminary, Michigan. She also has a social studies secondary education degree from Crown College, Minnesota in addition to Bible from Vennard College.

Sue has served in various teaching capacities both overseas in S. Korea and Mongolia, as well as in inter-city Detroit. She has travelled extensively both internationally and throughout the United States and Canada.

Sue was raised in a pastor's home where money did not always abound, yet personal sacrifice was taught at an early age. Sue and her siblings were exposed to inter-city rescue missions, Indian reservations, and low-income homes which housed the children on the church bus route. As an adult she received complete exposure to third world countries where the needs were more than overwhelming and God's call for giving became abundantly clear.

Sue and her husband currently live in Ohio with their two children. They are actively involved within their church in the areas of missions and outreach both locally and abroad. Much of their free time is spent generating extra income to send to overseas ministries where the needs are great and the resources are extremely limited.